St. Teresa of Avila's

NINE GRADES
of PRAYER

SCIENCE *of* SAINTHOOD

SCIENCE *of* SAINTHOOD

Video Study Written by Matthew Leonard
Workbook Written by Matthew Leonard & Curtis Mitch

Cover Design and layout by Patty Borgman

Science Of Sainthood | **ScienceOfSainthood.com**

Table of Contents

Welcome to the Science of Sainthood

Welcome to *St. Teresa of Avila's Nine Grades of Prayer*, presented by the Science of Sainthood.

Founded by evangelist Matthew Leonard, the Science of Sainthood is one of the world's premier online Catholic communities dedicated to teaching authentic Catholic spirituality. Steeped in the tradition of Saints like John of the Cross, Teresa of Avila, and Thomas Aquinas, our goal is to guide regular Catholics, step by step, down the path to nothing less than sainthood.

More than education, this is *transformation*!

How to Use This Workbook

The fourteen lessons in this study—titled *St. Teresa of Avila's Nine Grades of Prayer*—is just one of many courses on Catholic spirituality you'll find at **ScienceOfSainthood.com**. Visit the site to learn more.

After the brief "Welcome to the Science of Sainthood" video, each subsequent lesson in this study contains the following sections:

- ◆ Short Introduction
- ◆ Review of the Previous Lesson
- ◆ Lesson Video
- ◆ Space to Take Notes on the Video Lesson
- ◆ A Passage from a Saint
- ◆ A Passage from Sacred Scripture for *Lectio Divina*
- ◆ Written Meditation
- ◆ Review & Discussion Questions
- ◆ Prayer Journal

How you use the sections depends completely on what works best for you and/or your group. The written sections are there for either group or individual use. Some groups simply discuss the video and leave the journaling and other content for use outside the group. Other groups work their way through each portion as a whole group, reading the passages aloud. Again, it's entirely up to your discretion.

Given the short duration of the initial video, we suggest your first meeting consists of watching the "Welcome to the Science of Sainthood" video and Lesson One.

As you can see, we have provided Review and Discussion Questions to help spur group discussion.

Aside from the "Welcome to the Science of Sainthood" video, each video is roughly 15 minutes long. This means it would be quite easy to do two lessons in one group study session. That said, the material is designed for flexibility. Use it in the manner most fitting for your group.

Finally, don't forget this study is just one of many within the Science of Sainthood.

If your parish does not have a subscription and you'd like information on how to enroll personally (or discover how your parish can enroll) in the Science of Sainthood, visit **ScienceOfSainthood.com**!

LESSON ONE

Overview and the First Grade of Prayer

Lesson Introduction

While all prayer essentially fits under the headings of vocal, meditative, and contemplative prayer, there's a lot more to it. St. Teresa of Avila draws much of this out in her famous Nine Grades of Prayer.

Beginning in this lesson, we're going to make our way through these Nine Grades in order to understand more deeply all the different levels and nuances of what we experience as we make our way up the divine ladder.

 PLAY VIDEO

Notes

_____

_____

_____

_____

_____

_____

_____

What The Saints Say

"'My daughter...why do you not tell me about everything that concerns you, even the smallest details? Tell Me about everything, and know that this will give Me great joy.' I answered, 'But You know about everything, Lord.'

And Jesus replied to me, 'Yes, I do know; but you should not excuse yourself with the fact that I know, but with childlike simplicity talk to Me about everything, for my ears and heart are inclined to you, and your words are dear to Me.'"

ST. FAUSTINA KOWALSKA — *20th century Polish nun & mystic whose apparitions inspired devotion to the divine mercy*

Lectio Divina

"And Mary said, 'My soul magnifies the Lord, and my spirit rejoices in God my Savior, for he has regarded the low estate of his handmaiden. For behold, henceforth all generations will call me blessed; for he who is mighty has done great things for me, and holy is his name.

And his mercy is on those who fear him from generation to generation. He has shown strength with his arm, he has scattered the proud in the imagination of their hearts, he has put down the mighty from their thrones, and exalted those of low degree; he has filled the hungry with good things, and the rich he has sent empty away.

He has helped his servant Israel, in remembrance of his mercy, as he spoke to our fathers, to Abraham and to his posterity for ever.'"

LUKE 1:46–55

Meditation

The story of the Visitation is a great reminder that Vocal Prayer never loses its significance and is beautifully powerful. First of all, upon hearing Mary's greeting, John the Baptist leaped in the womb of Elizabeth. Why? Because of the power of Mary's words. They communicated the Holy Spirit. And the joy of the unborn child was shared by his mother.

Luke tells us that Elizabeth "exclaimed with a loud cry" words that comprise a good portion of the second most famous vocal prayer after the Our Father, the Hail Mary. "Blessed are you among women, and blessed is the fruit of your womb!" (Luke 1:42).

But even more interesting is that the joyful response of Our Lady – the famous Magnificat - is exclaimed by perhaps the most meditative person in the history of the world (aside from Christ himself).

Immaculately conceived and in the deepest of communion with the Lord through the Holy Spirit, the Blessed Virgin Mary had already ascended the spiritual ladder. She was the kind of person who spent time "pondering...in her heart" (Luke 2:19).

In fact, Our Lady only speaks in four different passages in the Bible. In other words, she wasn't much of a talker.

And yet, in response to Elizabeth, this deeply meditative soul exclaims aloud how blessed she is and extols the Lord for his goodness and mercy to her. Why? Because even though she had scaled the spiritual heights, she was still human. And as a human, she felt the deep need to give voice to her joy. It flowed naturally.

And it should flow naturally for us, as well. Like Mary and Elizabeth, no matter how far into meditative or contemplative prayer we may be, vocal prayer always retains great power and significance. Just as we should never stop talking to those we love on earth, so we should never stop crying aloud to God.

Review Questions

1. Why is it important to understand the different levels of prayer? How can learning about these levels help you in a practical way?

2. What do the various "grades of prayer" enable us to climb, according to Saint Teresa of Avila?

3. The video distinguished between the *ascetical* phase of the spiritual life and the *mystical* phase. What are the differences between them? Who is most active in each phase?

4. What are the two things that Vocal Prayer requires of us to be meritorious?

Discussion Questions

1. It's true that prayer is a *duty* for Christians because all of us are called to mature in the spiritual life. But just like the duties that children have toward their parents, prayer is ultimately about a *relationship.* It's about strengthening the bond that unites us with our heavenly Father.

What can our personal relationships with spouses, family members, and friends teach us about growing closer to God?

2. Prayer can be very demanding on our frail human nature. Despite our best efforts, we often struggle to focus on what we're saying, and sometimes we even struggle to stay awake. What strategies have you found most helpful in minimizing distractions and in making your conversation with the Lord focused and heartfelt?

Prayer Journal

LESSON TWO

General Meditation – Second of the Nine Grades of Prayer

What We Covered in Our Last Lesson

In the first lesson, we looked at spiritual progress in prayer. We examined the rungs of the divine ladder, the Nine Grades of Prayer, which lead us into deeper union with God. Along the way, we noted that the Nine Grades of Prayer are closely connected with the three modes, or categories of prayer—vocal, meditative, and contemplative. In fact, the Nine Grades outlined by St. Teresa are stages of progress within these three modes.

Next, we saw that the Nine Grades identify two overarching phases of the spiritual life. The first four grades of prayer make up the ascetical phase, and the five grades that follow make up the mystical phase. In the ascetical phase, we're the active ones. We commit ourselves to learning the basics of prayer, such as how to meditate well, and we're working diligently to rid our lives of vice and fill them with virtue.

In the mystical phase, the situation is reversed. This is where souls in love with God move into Infused Contemplation. At this level, God is the impetus for prayer and the One who acts within us. We don't do anything except receive the infusion, the inflow of his Presence. It's all him. We can prepare ourselves for mystical communion with God by our ascetical practices, particularly meditative prayer and the practice of virtue, but only God can make infused prayer happen.

Finally, we considered the importance of Vocal Prayer as the first of the Nine Grades. This is the foundation of our communication with the Lord and always will be. It is never something we leave behind, even when we advance to higher stages. Vocal Prayer is particularly important in the liturgy. In fact, all things being equal, the Church's public prayer is more powerful and more glorifying to God than our private prayers. Still, Vocal Prayer is essential to our devotional lives as individuals.

In order to be truly and richly meritorious, spoken prayers should be offered with attention and devotion. Praying with attention means that our minds are fully awake and focused as much as possible on the words we're saying. The more focused we are, the more meritorious our prayer. Praying with devotion means that our wills are fervently engaged in giving homage and glory to the Lord, regardless of whether or not our emotions are stirred up in the process.

Lesson Introduction

While we saw that Vocal Prayer is something we never leave behind even as we ascend the divine ladder, meditation is, in many ways, the key to spiritual growth. Without it, we will never progress. As St. Alphonsus Liguori declared, "He who prays most receives most."

Notes

What the Saints Say

"We meditate before, during, and after everything we do. The prophet says: 'I will pray, and then I will understand.' This is the way we can easily overcome the countless difficulties we have to face day after day, which, after all, are part of our work...In meditation we find the strength to bring Christ to birth in ourselves and in others."

ST. CHARLES BORROMEO — *16th Century Cardinal Archbishop of Milan & leader of the Counter-Reformation against the Protestant "Reformation." Patron saint of bishops.*

Lectio Divina

"Blessed is the man who walks not in the counsel of the wicked,
   nor stands in the way of sinners,
   nor sits in the seat of scoffers;
but his delight is in the law of the Lord,
   and on his law he meditates day and night."

PSALM 1:1–2

Meditation

When reading a different language, it's easy to miss the full significance of translated words. For example, when we read the word "Blessed," we perhaps don't realize the intense pleasure with which it is associated. In Hebrew, "blessed" means "O the happiness of!" It's a great exclamation of joy! In other words, meditating upon the Word of God leads to ecstasy and elation. By contrast, *not* meditating upon it is a slippery slope to disaster.

Notice the progression of sin shown by the Psalmist in our *Lectio Divina* passage above. If we're not focused upon the Word of God, keeping it in our heart, we'll go from walking "in the counsel of the wicked," to standing "in the way of sinners," to finally sitting "with the scoffers."

To put it another way, if we don't spend time in the purity of meditative prayer and God's Word, we'll go from hanging out with the bad crowd, to engaging in frequent habitual sin, to flat out denial of God.

That's disaster.

But again, that's the negative side of things. We don't only meditate upon the Word of God to avoid sin. We do it to experience fulfillment and joy at *all* times in life. So, whether we're in the midst of a time of contentment or a difficult trial, as long as we're meditating upon the Lord, we remain "blessed"!

Review Questions

1. What is meditation, according to the video? How is meditation different from Vocal Prayer?

2. Who is the ultimate focus of meditation and why?

3. How do we prepare ourselves to engage in meditative prayer? What are some practical steps we might take before conversing with God?

4. Meditation involves more than silent listening. According to the video, "Prayer is about action." What does that mean, exactly?

5. Why is mental prayer so vital to the spiritual life? What happens when we make it an integral part of our lives? What, according to St. Alphonsus Liguori, happens to a person when mental prayer is abandoned?

Discussion Questions

1. St. Paul urges Christians to "pray without ceasing" (1 Thess 5:17). That sounds impossible. We have so many other duties and responsibilities that fill our days. Not even a cloistered monk can spend every twenty-four hours in uninterrupted communication with the Lord.

How, then, can the apostle's command be obeyed? What are some ways that our whole lives can be offered to God in a spirit of prayer?

2. St. Teresa of Avila teaches that "voluntary distraction" in prayer is a venial sin. Perhaps that surprises you. But think about it for a moment. Have you ever been annoyed, or even felt hurt, when you've spoken with someone who was distracted by a phone or a television?

What do you think God would say to someone whose attention was constantly pulled away from prayer? How can eliminating voluntary distractions be a sign of your love?

Prayer Journal

LESSON THREE

Affective Prayer – Third of the Nine Grades of Prayer

What We Covered in Our Last Lesson

Last time we looked at meditation, the second of the Nine Grades of Prayer. The practice of meditation, we learned, is foundational to our movement through the stages of the spiritual life. It's not something to be put off until later on. Meditation is basically supposed to start right away when we begin a dedicated life of prayer.

So, what is it? Meditation is attentive reflection on Our Lord that is aided by some kind of spiritual input. It's a form of quiet, interior prayer, in which a conversation takes place between you and God. And it's ultimately focused on Jesus Christ. Everything comes back to him because our goal is to become like him.

How do we actually engage in meditation? The video outlined some basics steps. You should prepare yourself for meditation by finding a time and place that are free from distractions; you should recollect yourself by placing yourself in the presence of God while blocking out the chaos of the world; and you should ask the Holy Spirit to help you.

Once these preparations are made, you begin by reading Scripture or a book of the Saints slowly and attentively. This is your input into the conversation. When the Lord brings something important to your attention, stop and engage it. Converse with the Lord about it. Then make a resolution to act upon what he shows you. Prayer, after all, is about action. It's about changing our lives. When the Lord reveals his will, ask him for the grace to do what he's asking you.

Finally, we learned that progress in the spiritual life, including progress through the Nine Grades of Prayer, is a long and slow process. Movement up the ladder of prayer doesn't happen overnight. If we're faithful, God will move us along at the speed which is best for us. At the same time, being content with the Lord's timing should not lead to complacency. The Catechism speaks of "The Battle of Prayer." It's a constant struggle against our fallen nature, as well as the Devil. That means we have to pray even when we don't feel like it, even when there are obstacles. That's the only way we're going to be conformed to Christ and become holy.

Lesson Introduction

It's time to move on to the third of the Nine Grades of Prayer – Affective Prayer. A form of regular meditation, Affective Prayer hones in on the incredible nature of God's love that paves the way for a deeper movement of the Holy Spirit in our soul.

Notes

What the Saints Say

"Prayer is the inner bath of love into which the soul plunges itself."

ST. JEAN MARIE BAPTISTE VIANNEY — *19th century French priest also known as the Curé of Ars. The patron saint of parish priests.*

Lectio Divina

"O that you would kiss me with the kisses of your mouth!
For your love is better than wine,
  your anointing oils are fragrant,
your name is oil poured out;
    therefore the maidens love you.
Draw me after you, let us make haste.
    The king has brought me into his chambers.
We will exult and rejoice in you;
    we will extol your love more than wine;
    rightly do they love you."

SONG OF SOLOMON 1:2–4

Meditation

The Song of Solomon is the pinnacle of romantic literature in the Hebrew Bible. It's a sonnet of desire in which Bridegroom and Bride cry out for one another. Their spousal relationship is an analogy of the covenant love between Israel and God, as well as the soul's deep desire for union with the Lord.

But, as with so many other passages of Scripture, there's more to this poetry than meets the eye. In the Jewish mystical tradition, the divine kiss – "O that you would kiss me with the kisses of your mouth!" – is far more than a reference to romantic longing.

The kiss of the Bridegroom is the kiss of death.

And while perhaps that seems a bit morbid, realize that ancient Jews regarded this kind of death as a moment of great ecstasy. In fact, "death by divine kiss," says Jewish scholar Michael Fishbane, "is seen as a sign of special favor, a mark of grace given to the saintly."[1]

But it wasn't given to everyone.

The passing from this life into the arms of God in the next required adherence to his law. "The rapturous death of the righteous by God culminates a lifetime of spiritual labor, of studying the Law and observing the commandments."[2]

And it's the same with us. In order for us to be found in the loving embrace of God at the end of our earthly life, we must throw ourselves into that union of love *now*. We can't expect a deep relationship with God for all eternity without sincerely committing ourselves to it from this moment on.

And prayer, of course, is a primary part of that commitment. Meditation focused upon the incredible love of God is the key to being found worthy of the divine kiss at the end of our earthly life.

[1] Fishbane, Michael., *The Kiss of God: Spiritual and Mystical Death in Judaism.* (Seattle: University of Washington Press). 1994 p. 18
[2] Ibid.

Review Questions

1. What is Affective Prayer? What do we start doing at this stage, according to St. Teresa, that makes it different from the preceding stage?

2. What two extremes should you avoid regarding Affective Prayer?

3. St. Teresa likens Affective Prayer to our Sunday rest. What does she mean by this comparison?

Discussion Questions

1. It might be helpful to remember that Affective Prayer is when we interiorly express our "affection" for the Lord in the midst of meditation. It's a subtle inspiration from the Holy Spirit to which we give consent and follow. Have you ever experienced a similar movement of affection and deepening of love in human relationships? If so, describe it.

2. According to the video, Affective Prayer requires input, typically in the form of spiritual reading. This is because "the will is a blind faculty that needs direction and enlightenment before it can love and desire the good" (Fr. Jordan Aumann). What saint books or devotional helps have you found most helpful in aiding your meditation? Are there any you would recommend for stirring up sentiments of love for God?

Prayer Journal

LESSON FOUR

The Prayer of Simplicity – Fourth of the Nine Grades of Prayer

What We Covered in Our Last Lesson

Last time we discussed Affective Prayer, those spontaneous moments in the midst of meditation when we cease from our reading and thinking and simply love the Lord with our wills. Affective Prayer is still a kind of meditation, and yet it's a distinct level. The primary difference is that in the Second Grade of Prayer (General Meditation), the intellect actively engages what we're reading. In other words, we're thinking and focusing on the content of our meditation.

But in Affective Prayer, our spiritual activity shifts from the intellect to the will. It's a transition in which love predominates and becomes the focus. Instead of thinking, trying to imagine details of particular Gospel scenes, or placing ourselves in the scenes themselves, we give ourselves over to loving the Lord for his boundless goodness and mercy.

To enter deeply into Affective Prayer, it's important to avoid extremes. That means we should avoid both *rushing* the transition from intellectual meditation to Affective Prayer as well as *resisting* it. On the one hand, we should be careful not to cease from the mental activity of meditation too quickly. On the other, we should not force ourselves to continue our meditation when the Holy Spirit's inspiration to love presents itself. When you feel a divine impulse to let go and love, embrace it. When the moment passes and your mind starts to wander, simply go back to your meditation.

You'll also recall that Affective Prayer still requires spiritual input, usually in the form of devotional reading. As we said, this type of prayer is an activity of the will. In other words, you're making a decision to do it. And yet Fr. Jordan Aumann says our will is a "blind" faculty that needs "direction and enlightenment." What he means is that an object of love must be set *before* the will in order to draw forth a movement of love *from* the will. That means books and other spiritual aids remain a necessary part of the Third Grade of prayer. By presenting us with Christ and his mercy, they show us the supreme object of our love and stimulate responses of love and gratitude.

Lastly, Affective Prayer begins a process in which our communication with God is becoming simplified. This process will not be complete until we reach the highest levels of contemplation; nevertheless, even at this stage we're starting to move toward a relationship with the Lord centered on simple love. It's a movement toward charity. And when charity (i.e. divine love) increases in us, everything good increases. So, when Affective Prayer is doing its job, we detach ourselves from the world more completely, we fulfill the duties of our state in life more faithfully, and we love Jesus Christ more ardently.

Lesson Introduction

First John 4:8 declares: "God is love." And we were created to be unified with him, in and *through* love. This full communion with the love of God is the culmination of the spiritual life.

As we progress in prayer, there comes a point in time when this love begins to strongly impress itself upon our heart and impact how we engage the Lord. Through a combination of practice and grace, we penetrate more easily into the sacred space occupied by our Lord in a simplified gaze of love.

Notes

_____

_____

_____

_____

_____

_____

What the Saints Say

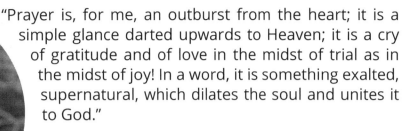

"Prayer is, for me, an outburst from the heart; it is a simple glance darted upwards to Heaven; it is a cry of gratitude and of love in the midst of trial as in the midst of joy! In a word, it is something exalted, supernatural, which dilates the soul and unites it to God."

ST. THERESE OF LISIEUX – *19th century Carmelite nun famous for her spirituality of the "Little Way"*

Lectio Divina

"O God, thou art my God, I seek thee,
   my soul thirsts for thee;
my flesh faints for thee,
   as in a dry and weary land where no water is.
So I have looked upon thee in the sanctuary,
   beholding thy power and glory.
Because thy steadfast love is better than life,
   my lips will praise thee.
So I will bless thee as long as I live;
   I will lift up my hands and call on thy name."

PSALM 63:1-8

Meditation

Though it's called the "Prayer of Simplicity," we have to remember that climbing the spiritual mountain is hard work. In order to get to the point where prayer is a "simple glance darted upwards to heaven" like St. Therese, we have to have developed a deep relationship with the Lord.

The key to this level of union is found in the first line of Psalm 63: "O God, you are my God, I *seek* you, my soul thirsts for you".

There you have it. We have to *seek* after the Lord with everything we possess. We must think of him upon our beds and meditate upon him "in the watches of the night" (63:6). Like any relationship, it is only upon spending serious time together that we can enter into a deep, simplified communion with the Lord.

And, eventually, this repeated act of the will to seek after the Lord is rewarded with a supreme sweetness of communion to which nothing in this world can compare. More of our soul is brought into union with the God who made us and who fills our heart to overflowing. Like Therese of Lisieux, Francis of Assisi, and so many other Saints, we become lost in his otherworldly love.

Review Questions

1. Saint Teresa of Avila refers to the Fourth Grade of prayer, the Prayer of Simplicity, as "acquired recollection." What do these two terms tell us about this kind of prayer?

2. Is the Prayer of Simplicity a form of meditation? How does this Fourth Grade of prayer differ from General Meditation (the Second Grade) and Affective Prayer (the Third Grade)?

3. Why does prayer become more simple as we progress?

Discussion Questions

1. The video cited St. Therese of Lisieux as saying: "The closer one approaches to God the simpler one becomes." How might this stress on simplicity help to explain what Jesus says in the Gospels: "Truly, I say to you, whoever does not receive the kingdom of God like a child shall not enter it." (Mark 10:15)?

2. St. Teresa of Avila encouraged her nuns to practice recollection. She knew that if they made a practice of focusing more upon God throughout the day it would help them move into his presence more quickly when they entered into their set time of regular prayer. What are some practical ways you can maintain focus upon the Lord throughout the day?

Prayer Journal

LESSON FIVE

Infused Contemplation, Part I – Fifth of the Nine Grades of Prayer

What We Covered in Our Last Lesson

In lesson four, we looked at the Prayer of Simplicity, which is the final step in our spiritual progress before we enter the realm of mystical prayer. We saw that, like Affective Prayer, this was a deeper level of meditation. It still takes place in the context of meditative prayer, and it still requires the input of spiritual reading. In other words, the Prayer of Simplicity still requires effort on our part, even though this effort is aided by grace. Unlike infused prayer, which comes next, it's something we have to work for.

We also saw that the Prayer of Simplicity is the most focused and unified form of meditation. It concentrates the powers of our intellect and will on a simple, spiritual gaze of love. An intensification of what began in Affective Prayer, the Prayer of Simplicity is a deeper "loving attention" we give to the Lord.

We also learned that prayer becomes simpler as we advance in the spiritual life because God is simple. He is the only Being whose essence and existence are one. In other words, unlike everyone and everything else, he doesn't need anyone or anything to give him life. He *is* life. He is also pure spirit, and so he has no body with parts and limbs. Therefore, when prayer becomes a more simple, intense, loving gaze, it begins to mirror the simplicity of God himself. Prayer at this level is tuned into him in a more perfect way and makes us more like him, which is the goal of the spiritual life.

What does this look like in practice? It starts with regular meditation using our spiritual reading (or whatever else we might use for input). When the Holy Spirit prompts us to stop reading and express our love, we're invited to move into Affective Prayer. Then, when the Spirit leads us to even more intense and deeper recollection, and we bring ourselves fully into God's presence, we're invited into the Prayer of Simplicity. This is when we focus our gaze, not on some particular aspect or perfection of God, but on the Divine Glory himself. St. Teresa says that at this point, the things of the world start to seem like insignificant "toys" compared to the gift of the Lord's majesty dwelling within us.

The Prayer of Simplicity is our final preparation before moving into Infused Contemplation.

Lesson Introduction

Having discussed both vocal and meditative prayer, we now move into the third main mode of prayer - contemplation. And it's a move that entails a transition from the natural to the supernatural, from the ascetical to the mystical. It's a brand-new experience of God in which we move into a relationship almost beyond words.

But as we're going to see, it's not something we can make happen on our own. While we have a role to play, a new level of relationship with the God of the universe can only happen through *his* power and in *his* timing.

Notes

What the Saints Say

"Contemplation is nothing else than a secret, peaceful, and loving infusion of God, which, if admitted, will set the soul on fire with the Spirit of love."

ST. JOHN OF THE CROSS — *16th century Carmelite mystic & Doctor of the Church*

Lectio Divina

"Behold, the days are coming, says the Lord, when I will make a new covenant with the house of Israel and the house of Judah, not like the covenant which I made with their fathers when I took them by the hand to bring them out of the land of Egypt, my covenant which they broke, though I was their husband, says the Lord. But this is the covenant which I will make with the house of Israel after those days, says the Lord: I will put my law within them, and I will write it upon their hearts; and I will be their God, and they shall be my people."

JEREMIAH 31:31–33

Meditation

To be in covenant with the Lord essentially means to be part of his family. And while the Israelites of the Old Testament had already become the "firstborn son" of God, the prophet Jeremiah prophesied about a "new covenant" that would change everything.

Of course, he's talking about the new covenant of Jesus Christ which took our relationship with God to a whole new level. United with Jesus, we literally become "sons in the Son," deified through the power of Christ.

And contemplative prayer plays a major role in that process of deification. It's a key to that new covenant relationship and our becoming "like Christ."

In fact, the Catechism of the Catholic Church says that "contemplative prayer is a covenant relationship established by Christ within our hearts." It's a "*communion* in which the Holy Trinity conforms man, the image of God, 'to his likeness'" (CCC 2713).

So contemplative prayer isn't just something we experience. It's something that *changes us*. As God pours himself into us, we become more and more like him. We see him more and more for who he is. And the more we see him, the more we love him.

Review Questions

1. What is Infused Contemplation? What makes this Fifth Grade of prayer different from the first four?

2. What can we do to bring about Infused Contemplation? Where does it actually come from?

3. Why is prayer increasingly difficult to describe as one moves through the Nine Grades?

4. Can we say that there are hard and fast lines between the different grades of prayer? Why or why not?

Discussion Questions

1. Every Christian is called to a life of progressive deification. What does it mean to be deified by grace? How is our life of prayer intertwined with this glorious calling?

2. The Nine Grades of Prayer are characterized by fluidity rather than rigidity. There are no hard-and-fast lines separating one stage from another. Instead, prayer is more like a rising tide: there's an overall movement toward higher ground, but there's plenty of ebb and flow in the midst of it.

Does this ring true of your own experience in prayer? Have you ever thought that some days you're gaining traction and other days you're backsliding? Should this always be a cause for worry?

Prayer Journal

LESSON SIX

Infused Contemplation, Part II – Mystical Movement & the Night of Sense

What We Covered in Our Last Lesson

Last time we were introduced to Infused Contemplation. Compared to the first Four Grades of prayer, the Fifth Grade of prayer is more supernatural. It imparts a more profound experience of God. It does so because it brings us across the threshold from ascetical prayer, where *we* do most of the work, to mystical prayer, where *God* takes the initiative and works within us. And as he grafts us more and more into his divine family, our soul can begin to experience "little tastes of heaven," profound experiences of God that go beyond the sensible consolations we may have experienced in meditative prayer.

We also learned that prayer at this level becomes difficult to describe. And this shouldn't be surprising. After all, we're moving from a more human, natural way to pray, to one solely powered by divine movement. God is beginning to pour himself into us. Put simply, we are being deified, prepared for our entrance into the Divine Family of God.

And it's because of this gradual movement into the divine that our words become less and less capable of capturing the reality of what is happening. Human language comes up against its limits when we begin to touch the supernatural. Saint Teresa herself acknowledged that infused prayer can seem "obscure" to those who've not yet experienced it.

That said, there are some basic things we can grasp. Infused Contemplation takes place when God pours his loving presence into a soul in a supernatural way. It's entirely an action of God that we can only receive. No technique or set of procedures can induce such an experience. Only God decides when infused prayer happens, and only God can make it happen.

Our job is to prepare ourselves to receive this gift. First, we must be in a state of grace. No one in a state of mortal sin can advance to the Fifth Grade of prayer. (A person constantly falling into mortal sin is going to have trouble progressing in prayer at all.)

Second, it is ordinarily the case that those who receive this infusion of God's love have been leading a dedicated life of prayer for some time. It generally comes to those who have long practiced meditation and faithfully committed themselves to growing in virtue. In other words, God bestows this gift of prayer on souls who have shown a strong and persistent desire to grow closer to him.

Lesson Introduction

When going through the Nine Grades of Prayer, we have to keep in mind that they fit into our overall movement through the three traditional stages of the spiritual life: the Purgative, Illuminative, and Unitive ways. (See the course titled, "The 3 Stages of the Spiritual Life" in ScienceOfSainthood.com.) These Nine Grades are different ways of talking about the same thing that complement the three stages. As we'll see in this lesson, our movement from ascetical prayer to mystical prayer (i.e., Infused Contemplation) is essentially part of the Night of Sense. It's part of our preparation for the second stage, the Illuminative Way.

Notes

What the Saints Say

"But there is another reason why God alone is the happiness of our souls, to which I wish rather to direct attention: The contemplation of Him, and nothing but it, is able fully to open and relieve the mind, to unlock, occupy, and fix our affections."

ST. JOHN HENRY NEWMAN (1801-1890) —
19th century cardinal and prolific author

Lectio Divina

"Blessed is the man who endures trial, for when he has stood the test, he will receive the crown of life which God has promised to those who love him."

JAMES 1:12

Meditation

As we discussed in this lesson, love is primarily an act of the will. That doesn't mean your emotions, feelings, and other senses in the "downstairs" of your soul aren't involved. They certainly are. But we all know that feelings come and go.

A long-married couple is well aware that "downstairs" butterflies don't constantly flutter. In fact, they know that not only are positive feelings fleeting, they're often replaced by *negative* feelings like anger, hurt, and frustration, as well. And yet, through it all, the bond of love remains strong. Why?

It's because the *decision* to love the other person, regardless of any relational hiccups, continues to mature. They've come to know and love each other deeply, and their relationship doesn't depend upon their emotional state.

And it's similar in our relationship with God.

The more we know the Lord and follow the promptings to make a gift of ourselves to him no matter what we feel (or don't feel), the deeper our divine intimacy. This is essentially the movement of prayer. It is an intensification of our loving knowledge of God. Prayer enables us to act on the grace offered by the Lord and have the firm will to follow him into the "upstairs" intimacy for which he longs.

And the beauty is that once we let go of our desire for sensible consolations and follow him upstairs, he rewards us with an intimacy that far exceeds the butterflies we used to enjoy in the early days of our relationship.

Review Questions

1. How are the Nine Grades of Prayer related to the three stages of the spiritual life taught by many saints, i.e., the Purgative, Illuminative, and Unitive ways? What does this relationship help us to see clearly about the life of prayer?

2. When we approach the realm of mystical prayer or Infused Contemplation, we begin to experience what St. John of the Cross calls the "Night of Sense." What is the Night of Sense and what feelings can accompany it?

3. The video describes the Night of Sense as an invitation from God to ascend from the "downstairs" of the soul to the "upstairs." What faculties of the soul live in the "downstairs" and "upstairs", respectively?

4. Why does God invite us "upstairs" in the Night of Sense? What is he trying to accomplish in us spiritually?

Discussion Questions

1. Saint Paul says that faithful Christians "walk by faith, not by sight" (2 Cor 5:7). He means that our life is directed by heavenly things we can neither see nor touch nor taste. In order to follow Christ faithfully, we have to think and make choices without the benefit of sense experience.

In view of what we've learned about the Night of Sense, how might the apostle's words that we "walk by faith, not by sight" apply to the life of prayer?

2. Many of us have probably experienced times of dryness in prayer. Has this happened to you? If so, how would you describe that experience? Did you worry that God was unhappy with you and growing distant from you? How does today's lesson challenge you to view spiritual dryness and aridity differently?

Prayer Journal

LESSON SEVEN

Infused Contemplation, Part III – Up and Down the Mountain of God

What We Covered in Our Last Lesson

Last time we took a step back to look at the big picture. We saw that the Nine Grades of Prayer overlay the three stages of spiritual growth: the Purgative, the Illuminative, and the Unitive ways. In a sense, we weren't really talking about different things. The "grades" and the "stages" are different ways of talking about the same thing. That said, the distinction draws our attention to an important point, namely, that growth in prayer and progress in the spiritual life are bound tightly together. They are part and parcel of the same thing.

Much of what we discussed concerns the shift from ascetical to mystical prayer, also known as Infused Contemplation. And it's during this transition that we can experience what St. John of the Cross calls the "Night of Sense." This is when God begins to feel distant because he begins to withhold some of the spiritual consolations that sweetened our experience of prayer in the earlier stages. Often this leads to a feeling of dryness, an aridity in prayer, as if God were pulling back from us or dimming the light of his presence. This can cause us to feel anxious and, if misunderstood, can even stop us from making spiritual progress.

The reality, however, is rather different. God is actually drawing closer in the Night of Sense—so close, in fact, that our senses, emotions, and imagination are blinded by his glory. We haven't yet developed the spiritual vision to sense his closeness.

In the Night of Sense, God is beginning to ask us to seek him for his own sake and not for the sake of the spiritual comforts we used to enjoy. In effect, the Lord is calling us to leave behind our reliance on the lower faculties that reside in the "downstairs" of our soul and ascend to the "upstairs" of the souls where our higher faculties, the intellect and will, can direct more of our prayer. This is a step toward progress and maturity in prayer because it enables us to know and love God in a more intense and spiritual way.

Lesson Introduction

In our final foray into the fifth grade of St. Teresa's Nine Grades of Prayer, we'll discuss what is meant by the unusual phrase "experimental knowledge" of God that occurs at this level of prayer. This will lead us to some very practical considerations. In particular, we'll answer the question of what our prayer life actually looks like at this stage of spiritual development.

Notes

_____

_____

_____

_____

_____

_____

_____

_____

_____

_____

_____

_____

What the Saints Say

"The greatness of contemplation can be given to none but those who love."

POPE ST. GREGORY THE GREAT — *6th century pope & originator of Gregorian chant*

Lectio Divina

"Now about eight days after these sayings he took with him Peter and John and James, and went up on the mountain to pray. And as he was praying, the appearance of his countenance was altered, and his raiment became dazzling white. And behold, two men talked with him, Moses and Elijah, who appeared in glory and spoke of his departure, which he was to accomplish at Jerusalem."

LUKE 9:29–31

Meditation

One of the most interesting details of the Transfiguration story is when Moses and Elijah appear with Christ in glory and speak about his "departure." In Greek, the word "departure" is *exodos*, which conjures up obvious parallels between Moses and Christ. Just as Moses led the Israelites out of the slavery of Egypt in the first exodus, so Christ leads the Church, the New Israel, out of the slavery of sin in a new exodus.

But there's a personal lesson here, as well.

In ancient Greek dramas, an *exodos* was the final scene in a play, particularly in a tragedy. Scholars throughout the ages have thus taken the word "departure" (*exodos*) in Luke 9:31 as a reference to the tragically beautiful event of the Lord's Passion and death.

So, while the veil of heaven was lifted ever so slightly and the glory of Christ was revealed at the Transfiguration, we learn what it takes to *achieve* this glory. In order to experience a personal "transfiguration" and participate in his divine nature, we must first follow Christ's lead. We must go through a personal *exodos*, a personal death to self.

And this is no once-and-done event. Our *exodos* is a *daily* carrying of our cross. We must use it to crush the vices that keep us chained to this world. That's what the spiritual life is all about.

And while our new exodus can at times feel like we're in a wilderness similar to the first exodus of the Israelites, don't ever forget the reward. We die to ourselves daily so as to rise with Christ for all eternity. "If we have been united with him in a death like his," declares St. Paul, "we shall certainly be united with him in a resurrection like his" (Romans 6:5).

Review Questions

1. When we reach the level of mystical, contemplative prayer, do we leave behind vocal and meditative prayer? If not, how do they continue to play a role in our life of prayer?

2. When we receive the gift of Infused Contemplation, do we remain in that *state*?

3. What is the practice of *Lectio Divina*? Can you name the four steps involved?

Discussion Questions

1. Have you ever seriously attempted *Lectio Divina*? What parts or passages of Scripture did you find most enriching for your prayer? If it's not something you've tried by following the traditional four steps, what's holding you back?

2. How might knowing the overall story of the Bible and it's cast of characters enrich your practice of *Lectio Divina*?

3. We've learned that progress in prayer is a lifelong commitment. It's a marathon rather than a sprint. That said, St. Teresa of Avila identifies "humility" as the inside lane, the path of shortest distance to the finish line. Why do you think humility is such a powerhouse virtue in the Christian life? Where do we see it in action in the lives of Jesus and Mary in the Gospels?

Prayer Journal

LESSON EIGHT

Prayer of Quiet, Part I – Captivating the Will & Active Contemplation

What We Covered in Our Last Lesson

In the last lesson, we filled out our understanding of Infused Contemplation. We were reminded that, for the most part, neither Vocal Prayer nor meditative prayer are left behind when we enter the realm of contemplative prayer. Vocal Prayer will always be a part of our spiritual life. This is true especially because participation in the Church's liturgy is an ongoing part of our lives.

Meditation will likely continue a role in our lives of prayer since it typically sets the stage for contemplative prayer. In rare cases, however, where a soul has made significant progress in the Unitive way, meditation may eventually become unnecessary.

We also examined what contemplation actually looks like in practical terms. And it was discussed that even when a person has entered the contemplative state, the mystical experience that can accompany it is *limited* to a set period of time determined by the Lord. It starts and it stops. It's not like we're in some kind of constant ecstasy.

Even so, contemplation has lasting effects that continue to shape and mold us. That's because once there, we've reached a new plateau in the spiritual life. Regardless of how long a person experiences a particular mystical infusion of divine love, once in the contemplative state, he or she will continue to grow more recollected and make progress toward God.

This lesson was nicely illustrated by the story of the Transfiguration. Peter, James, and John, the disciples who climbed up the mountain with Jesus, had a profound contemplative experience. They gazed upon the glory of God in Jesus Christ, but only for a limited time. Nevertheless, it changed them in a lasting way. Even after they descended the mountain and re-engaged the rest of the world, they remained close to the Lord. They continued to walk with Jesus and to work for God's kingdom alongside him.

Finally, we learned a "shortcut" for advancing in the spiritual life. There is no question that developing a prayerful relationship with the Lord is a lifelong pursuit. But, according to St. Teresa of Avila, the shortest route to progress passes through the virtue of humility. In her own remarkable words: "It is by humility that the Lord allows Himself to be conquered so that He will do all we ask of Him."

Lesson Introduction

In the sixth of the Nine Grades of Prayer—the Prayer of Quiet—we begin to see the contours of real Catholic spirituality. This is the level where Mary and Martha are beautifully blended in a life of true and active contemplation. Why?

Because God has totally captivated our will and drawn us even closer.

Notes

What the Saints Say

"We ascend to the heights of contemplation by the steps of action."

POPE ST. GREGORY THE GREAT — *6th century pope & originator of Gregorian chant*

Lectio Divina

"Now as they went on their way, he entered a village; and a woman named Martha received him into her house. And she had a sister called Mary, who sat at the Lord's feet and listened to his teaching. But Martha was distracted with much serving; and she went to him and said, 'Lord, do you not care that my sister has left me to serve alone? Tell her then to help me.'

But the Lord answered her, 'Martha, Martha, you are anxious and troubled about many things; one thing is needful. Mary has chosen the good portion, which shall not be taken away from her.'"

LUKE 10:38–42

Meditation

What is the main difference between Martha and Mary in this famous story of Jesus' visit to Martha's house? It's certainly not that Martha's service to the Lord was wrong. In fact, St. Augustine points out that in this story "a servant received her Lord, the sick her Saviour, the creature her Creator."[1]

Receiving the Lord into the home of our hearts is exactly what each of us is supposed to do. In fact, feeding the hungry is one of the corporal works of mercy. Martha's action is a fundamental part of being a Christian.

But, still, says the Lord, "Mary has chosen the good portion, which shall not be taken away from her." What is it that makes Mary's choice the "good" (or "better" as some translations render it) portion? Why does the Lord extol her?

It's because, while Martha worked to feed our Lord, "Mary her sister chose rather to be fed *by* the Lord," says Augustine.[2] Perhaps this is why Martha was so anxious. Her desire to work was good, but apparently it wasn't properly ordered. Put simply, work needs to be preceded by prayer. First, we are to sit at the feet of the Lord; *then* we are empowered to work. And it's not just that prayer empowers us to work on earth. It will outlast everything we do in this life, as well.

"The works of an active life pass away with the body," says St. Gregory the Great, "but the joys of the contemplative life...begin to increase from the end."[3] So like Mary, may we always keep our priorities straight and choose the "good portion" ...the *eternal* portion.

[1] Thomas Aquinas. (1843). *Catena Aurea: Commentary on the Four Gospels, Collected out of the Works of the Fathers: St. Luke.* (J. H. Newman, Ed.) (Vol. 3, p. 378). Oxford: John Henry Parker.

[2] Ibid

[3] Ibid., page 382

Review Questions

1. What is meant by the Prayer of Quiet? Why is it challenging to describe?

2. What part of the soul is the focus at the *beginning* of the Prayer of Quiet? (Note: What happens as the Prayer of Quiet progresses will be the subject of our next lesson.)

3. How does the Prayer of Quiet affect our daily lives and routines outside of our devotional times? In other words, once in this grade of prayer, what does life now look like practically speaking?

Discussion Questions

1. Much of what we do depends on our motivation. Put another way, do we do something because we *have* to, or because we *want* to? How do you think a motivation of love would change things in your day to day life? Would it change how you go about your duties? How might it impact your life of prayer?

2. Oftentimes we have a fear of losing control of ourselves even in the slightest degree. And yet, being conformed to God in prayer implies a yielding of our will to his. Does the idea of your will being "captivated" by God make you nervous or appeal to you?

3. Martha and Mary represent the active and contemplative sides of the spiritual life—Mary, the life of quiet prayer; and Martha, the life of practical service. Do you identify more closely with Martha or Mary? Why did Jesus say that Mary chose the better portion? How does this lesson help you understand how these two sides of the Christian life are meant to blend together?

Prayer Journal

LESSON NINE

Prayer of Quiet, Part II – Holy Heavenly Madness & the Inebriation of Love

What We Covered in Our Last Lesson

Last time we continued our discussion of mystical prayer by looking at the sixth of the Nine Grades, the Prayer of Quiet. And, again, we were reminded of the difficulty of describing these higher levels of communion with the Lord. The words of the Saints can give us a basic sense of what's happening, but human words in general struggle to express the magnificence of it all.

That said, a few distinctions can help us understand things a bit. We've said before that mystical prayer is when God invites us into the "upstairs" of our soul where the intellect and will, our higher faculties, have their home. First we saw the movement toward the *will* in Affective Prayer. Then God's attention shifted toward the *intellect* beginning in the Prayer of Simplicity and continuing in Infused Contemplation.

But the Lord's work isn't done.

In the beginning of the Prayer of Quiet, he shifts the focus of his activity from the intellect back to the will. Now that we're "upstairs," God seizes our will with his love, so that our will and his are more closely united. And the result of this deeper union of our will with his is that we live our daily lives with greater intensity. Everything we do, no matter how mundane, is done with an ardent love for God.

What is happening is that prayer and life are becoming one. It's as though Mary and Martha, the sisters who appear in the Gospels, are merging together. Martha, you'll remember, served the Lord in an *active* way; she attended to all the practical needs that hosting Jesus in her home required. Mary, however, chose the better portion by following a *contemplative* way. Instead of busying herself with preparations, she sat attentively at Jesus's feet.

In a sense, the responses of these two sisters begin to blend together in the Prayer of Quiet. Once we've taken the time to listen quietly to the Lord as the honored Guest of our soul, we are filled with a spiritual zeal for serving him in all that we do. In the video, Matthew referred to this as "active contemplation."

Lesson Introduction

In finishing our discussion of the sixth of the Nine Grades of Prayer, the Prayer of Quiet, we'll learn about the incredible consolations that accompany this stage. They're known as the "sleep of the faculties" in which Fr. Jordan Aumann says, God "fills the soul and body with ineffable sweetness and delight." As you can imagine, it's a level of consolation that almost defies description.

Notes

What the Saints Say

"Sometimes, in prayer, God communicates to the soul, all at once, His treasures of lights and heavenly graces. Imagine that you have in your hand a golden dish, that you pour into it the extract of the rarest and most exquisite perfumes, and that you steep into it a fine cambric handkerchief; this handkerchief will yield a delicious and inexplicable odor, composed of all the perfumes. It is thus my soul feels when I receive those intimate and hidden communications."

ST. PAUL OF THE CROSS — *18th century founder of the Congregation of the Passion of Jesus Christ (the Passionists)*

Lectio Divina

"I slept, but my heart was awake.
Hark! my beloved is knocking.
'Open to me, my sister, my love,
    my dove, my perfect one;
for my head is wet with dew,
    my locks with the drops of the night.'
I had put off my garment,
    how could I put it on?
I had bathed my feet,
    how could I soil them?
My beloved put his hand to the latch,
    and my heart was thrilled within me."

SONG OF SOLOMON 5:2–4

Meditation

Why is it that the Lord so generously fills us with his divine presence on this side of heaven? Why does he allow us to experience something so overwhelmingly incredible as the "sleep of the faculties" as we progress into his presence?

Certainly, there's a sense in which it is a foreshadowing of our final end. These consolations are tastes of the eternal joy of heaven itself.

As we've noted several times before, this is exactly what was experienced by three of the disciples at the Transfiguration when the veil of heaven was drawn back ever so slightly and they were dazzled by the divinity of Christ.

But as St. Bede the Venerable (8th century English Benedictine monk) points out, the consolations tasted by the disciples were not an end in themselves. Jesus, "In loving concession, allowed Peter, James and John to enjoy for a very short time the contemplation of happiness that lasts forever, so as to enable them to bear adversity with greater fortitude."

In other words, God always acts with a purpose. The intermittent consolations we experience from the Lord are always meant to help us persevere through a world that is darkened by sin and suffering. He's allowing us to enjoy the final glory of being united to the Cross of Jesus Christ even though we're not yet there.

And at the end of the day, it's all simply a movement of intensifying love in which the *supernatural* glories of life with Christ stand in sharper relief against the background of even the greatest *natural* goods.

These otherworldly consolations increase our desire for the Lord and help us exclaim along with St. Paul, "I count everything as loss because of the surpassing worth of knowing Christ Jesus my Lord. For his sake I have suffered the loss of all things, and count them as refuse, in order that I may gain Christ" (Philippians 2:8).

Review Questions

1. In the Prayer of Quiet, God first captivates the will, then captivates the intellect and other faculties with delights beyond description. How are the spiritual consolations that come in the Prayer of Quiet different from those experienced in earlier levels of prayer?

2. How does St. Teresa describe these consolations of the Prayer of Quiet?

3. What happens after the Prayer of Quiet ends and the soul returns to daily life? How does the experience affect our level of satisfaction in the goods of this life?

Discussion Questions

1. When St. Paul bursts out in praise in his Letter to the Ephesians, he says of God: "Now to him who by the power at work within us is able to do far more abundantly than all that we ask or think, to him be glory in the Church and in Christ Jesus to all generations, for ever and ever. Amen."

What are some ways that Paul's prayer becomes a reality in the Prayer of Quiet? Does understanding this incredible movement of God in our soul at this level stir your spirit to seek after the Lord?

2. Does this lesson help you begin to understand why so many biblical characters and saints seem to almost burst with joy in the presence of God? Who are some other examples of biblical characters that exclaimed aloud at God's work in their lives?

3. St. Teresa is adamant that the Prayer of Quiet is God's doing. He is the one who acts within us and determines how long this experience of mystical communion will last. We cannot make it happen; we can only prepare ourselves to receive it. For St. Teresa, we make ourselves ready by "humility" and a "desire to suffer." These are certainly characteristics and desires that are impossible to acquire on our own. They happen through grace.

Even so, why do you think these are the essential ingredients for serious growth in the spiritual life? What is being asked of us?

Prayer Journal

LESSON TEN

Prayer of Union, Part I – Captives of God

What We Covered in Our Last Lesson

In the last lesson, we finished our study of the Prayer of Quiet, the Sixth Grade of prayer. We learned that, as this stage unfolds, God first captivates our will and then captivates our intellect as well. As in meditative prayer, the prayer of auiet brings spiritual consolations, but now they're different. *We* worked for the consolations experienced in meditation; now *God* gives them to us as pure gifts. Beyond that, the consolations and delights of the Prayer of Quiet are of much greater magnitude. St. Teresa speaks of them as "the greatest peace and quietness and sweetness within ourselves."

Describing what takes place in the Prayer of Quiet is challenging because we're talking about something that touches the very center of the soul. And it does so in a way that the soul itself cannot understand. St. Teresa likens it to a fragrant smoke and heat that penetrates the entire soul and even touches the body. This leads to a state of "heavenly madness" in which the soul, barely able to contain itself, pours out a torrent of praises to the Lord. It's an experience of God that's beyond words.

The effect of the Prayer of Quiet upon our personal lives is tremendous. No one who reaches this level is left unchanged. Souls who have tasted God's finer delights no longer take comfort in the pleasures of the world. Even things as basic as eating and sleeping become far less satisfying—almost burdensome, in fact— because the soul comes to a deeper realization that God alone can satisfy. In other words, in the Prayer of Quiet, the Lord helps us to become more detached from the comforts of this life and more desirous of him alone.

According to St. Teresa, the tension of living in the world but yearning to leave it behind for a more complete union with God is actually a cross. It's a light cross because of the sweetness it brings. But it's also a heavy cross because it's hard to endure. When God begins to bless the soul with such exquisite tokens of love, it can only want more. The key is to focus our desire on God himself and not on the gifts he bestows.

Lesson Introduction

As incredible as the Prayer of Quiet is, the Prayer of Union is a completely different level. As the title indicates, it's our move into the Unitive Way, the third and final stage of the spiritual life. And as you can imagine, there's a lot happening in both body and spirit. Put simply, God is taking over...and it's an incredibly beautiful thing.

 PLAY VIDEO

Notes

What the Saints Say

"Prayer is nothing else than union with God. When the heart is pure and united with God it is consoled and filled with sweetness; it is dazzled by a marvelous light."

ST. JEAN MARIE BAPTISTE VIANNEY — *19th century French priest also known as the Curé of Ars. The patron saint of parish priests.*

Lectio Divina

"'Jesus then said, 'I shall be with you a little longer, and then I go to him who sent me; you will seek me and you will not find me; where I am you cannot come.' The Jews said to one another, 'Where does this man intend to go that we shall not find him? Does he intend to go to the Dispersion among the Greeks and teach the Greeks? What does he mean by saying, 'You will seek me and you will not find me,' and, 'Where I am you cannot come'"?

JOHN 7:32–36

Meditation

Why is it that Jesus tells the crowd in John 7 that "'You will seek me and you will not find me,' and, 'Where I am you cannot come'"? After all, isn't that what the spiritual life is all about? Aren't we seeking Christ so as to unify ourselves with him?

Yes, we certainly are. So why does Christ seem to make the effort sound futile? Well, the reality is that he's not saying what it looks like on the surface. There's a deeper meaning.

The great fourth-century Church Father, St. Augustine, explains at least part of what Christ is telling us. "He does not say, Where I shall be, but *Where I am*. For Christ was always there in that place whither He was about to return." In other words, Augustine says that Christ was telling his listeners that, as the God-man, he was on earth and in heaven at the same time. Realize that there was never a time when the Second Person of the Holy Trinity was not present to the other Persons of the Trinity.

Jesus was always God, even on earth.

So, when he said that the people could not go where he was, he meant heaven. "Visibly and according to the flesh, He was upon earth," says Augustine, "according to His invisible majesty, He was in heaven and earth."

Of course, we know that though we're moving toward union, we cannot yet fully join God while we're still on earth. Even so, his promise is that one day – provided we live in and through Him – he'll bring us into *full* communion with him for all eternity. "And when I go and prepare a place for you," says Christ, "I will come again and will take you to myself, that where I am you may be also" (John 14:3).

That's the *real* communion for which we're striving. The reason the Prayer of Union is so incredibly sweet and desirable is because it's a tiny foretaste of our eternal union with Jesus. In other words, we would be crazy to stop praying and seeking after God!

Review Questions

1. Name the final three levels of the Nine Grades of Prayer. How are they similar?

2. What makes the Prayer of Union, the Seventh Grade of prayer, different from the Prayer of Quiet that preceded it? And how does what happens in this level of prayer affect our ability to focus on God?

3. Are the ecstasies we experience in the Prayer of Union continuous? In other words, once we reach this level can we still function "normally" in life and fulfill our natural duties?

Discussion Questions

1. It's impossible to imagine the unimaginable. St. Teresa even says that no comparison with earthly things can explain the mystical experiences of the final grades of prayer. The best we can do is insist that they far surpass the greatest natural pleasures we've ever experienced.

2. Have you ever experienced "spiritual" joys in your life that affected you more deeply than "natural" pleasures? If so, explain.

3. Jesus teaches his disciples in the Gospel: "Whoever would save his life will lose it, and whoever loses his life for my sake will find it" (Matthew 16:25). It's easy to see how this passage could apply to martyrdom and the eternal life that follows. But can you also see a connection between Christ's words and the higher levels of prayer?

Prayer Journal

LESSON ELEVEN

Prayer of Union, Part II – The Wounds of Love

What We Covered in Our Last Lesson

Last time we began our study of the Prayer of Union, the Seventh Grade of prayer. And we saw that even the delights of the Prayer of Quiet, as amazing as they are, cannot compare to the ecstasies and consolations of the Prayer of Union. At this point, the soul has arrived at a level of mystical experience that no one can really describe, and no comparison with earthly realities can really help us understand.

The Prayer of Union is among the uppermost levels of prayer. In this study on the Nine Grades of Prayer, the final three grades are called the Prayer of Union, the Prayer of Conforming Union, and the Prayer of Transforming Union. We distinguish these three stages and give them separate labels, but it's important to remember they're all part of the same movement. All three are technically the same level of prayer. We're basically talking about degrees of intensity. A soul that is this close to God has reached the final stage of its journey and is being flooded with Divine Life in astounding ways.

One way to get a handle on "what's new" about the Seventh Grade of prayer is to compare it with the Sixth. In the Prayer of Quiet, the Lord began by captivating the will with his love and continued by captivating the intellect as well. You'll recall that the memory and imagination were still free to roam at this stage.

In this next stage, the Prayer of Union, the Lord extends his reach over us even more by also captivating the memory and imagination. The only thing now free are our bodily senses. Put simply, God is continuing to "take over" as he draws us ever closer.

Saint Teresa describes this mystical state in various ways. She says the soul rejoices in some "good thing" but without comprehending that good thing. One is overcome with joy, but there is no power left in body or soul to express this joy. Our bodily functions seem paralyzed, totally asleep to the things of the world, and even the soul is without the conscious ability to think. One merely "rests" in the peace of supernatural joy.

Lesson Introduction

While describing the Prayer of Union can be a bit murky given its highly mystical, otherworldly character, there are some specific signs that help determine whether or not a person has experienced it.

Additionally, because we are experiencing an incredibly deep union with the Lord, some very amazing things can start to happen. In fact, Saints Teresa of Avila and John of the Cross identify four different phenomena associated with this stage of prayer.

Notes

What the Saints Say

"I am the wheat of God and am ground by the teeth of the wild beasts, that I may be found the pure bread of God. I long after the Lord, the Son of the true God and Father, Jesus Christ. Him I seek, who died for us and rose again. I am eager to die for the sake of Christ. My love has been crucified, and there is no fire in me that loves anything. But there is living water springing up in me, and it says to me inwardly: 'Come to the Father.'"

ST. IGNATIUS OF ANTIOCH — *Early Christian Bishop and Martyr*

Lectio Divina

"Little children, yet a little while I am with you. You will seek me; and as I said to the Jews so now I say to you, 'Where I am going you cannot come.' A new commandment I give to you, that you love one another; even as I have loved you, that you also love one another. By this all men will know that you are my disciples, if you have love for one another."

Simon Peter said to him, 'Lord, where are you going?' Jesus answered, 'Where I am going you cannot follow me now; but you shall follow afterward.' Peter said to him, 'Lord, why cannot I follow you now? I will lay down my life for you.' Jesus answered, 'Will you lay down your life for me? Truly, truly, I say to you, the cock will not crow, till you have denied me three times.'"

JOHN 13:33–38

Meditation

It's a question that arises time and time again. Why are so many Catholics more than willing to suffer and die for the faith? What's the secret to that yearning for trials, and even death, that we see in the lives of Saints like Ignatius of Antioch?

The secret, as we're starting to see more and more, is nothing other than intimate union with the Lord. And the only way to truly follow Christ and be unified with him is through the Cross. That's the font from which the power to live and love like Christ comes. That's the essence of our union.

It's easy to get caught up in the amazing consolations that accompany the higher levels of prayer. But we have to remember that they are simply the fruit of a life lived in sacrificial union with the Lord. They are fruit borne out of suffering.

As St. Paul of the Cross says, "Souls who aspire to a sublime union with God by contemplation usually suffer interior purgations in one way or another."

And yet, it's not a miserable life. It's a life of *love*. It's a desperate desire to give of ourselves like Christ because we're becoming more and more like him. We acquire an ever-deepening desire that the entire world be joined to Jesus in the same way that we are, and we are willing to offer ourselves in suffering love in order to see that happen. And we also come to realize more and more that the *only* way salvation comes is through the Cross.

As St. Therese of Lisieux wrote in *The Story of a Soul*, "One cannot attain the end without adopting the means, and as Our Lord made me understand that it was by the Cross He would give me souls, the more crosses I met with the stronger grew my attraction to suffering."

Put simply, salvation comes through union with the Cross of Christ...period.

But rather than pain and misery, it's a life of suffering *love* empowered by the amazing grace won by what Our Lord has already accomplished through that same Cross. Jesus has already done all the heavy lifting. That's why he can promise us, "My yoke is easy, and my burden is light" (Matthew 11:30).

Review Questions

1. In the video, Matthew compared the Prayer of Union to God reversing the aging process. What does he mean by this?

2. It's not unusual for a person to wonder whether they've reached the Prayer of Union and whether their spiritual experiences are real. What are three "signs" that help to authenticate the Prayer of Union?

3. How long does the Prayer of Union last?

4. Can you name the four phenomena that often accompany the Prayer of Union according to Saints such as Teresa of Avila and John of the Cross?

Discussion Questions

1. The Prayer of Union reminds us how little we actually know of God. There is no way the immensity of his divinity can be comprehended by our limited minds. He cannot be solved and set aside like a 1000-piece puzzle or a Rubix Cube.

Do you find this humbling fact encouraging or discouraging? If you're married, do you take delight in discovering new things about your spouse, even if you've been together for decades? How might deep relationships with other humans help us understand, in a small way, the boundless mystery of God?

2. Saint John of the Cross says that the Prayer of Union reveals the holiness of God's name in a whole new way. What does it mean to say that the Lord's name is "holy"? Jesus instructs us in the Our Father that God's name should be "hallowed" (Matthew 6:9). How do we do that, practically speaking?

ıyer Journal

PRAYER

Prayer of Conforming Union, Part I – The Ecstasy of Spiritual Betrothal

What We Covered in Our Last Lesson

Last time we continued our study of the Prayer of Union. We learned that, at this point, we've entered the third stage of the spiritual life, the Unitive Way. As Matthew described it in the video, it's as though God is reversing the aging process. With all of our interior faculties captivated by the Lord, our control over various aspects of our natural life is waning. God is creating us anew, remaking us in his image and likeness. He is helping us to become like little children who are totally dependent on him.

We also examined the question: How do you know if what you're experiencing is the Prayer of Union? Basically, there are three "signs" that serve as tests. First, at this level of prayer, there are *no distractions*. Distractions are usually stirred up by our memory and imagination, but now these interior faculties have been captivated by the Lord and so they are firmly under his control.

Second, the soul has *no doubt* about being in communion with God. The questions and suspicions that often arise in the Prayer of Quiet – the previous grade of prayer - give way to total certainty in the Prayer of Union.

Third, the soul experiences *no fatigue*. Earlier forms of prayer can leave one feeling weary and drained, but this goes away in the Prayer of Union, no matter how long it lasts.

Among the spiritual phenomena that accompany the Prayer of Union, we saw that Teresa of Avila and John of the Cross describe four. The first is *mystical touch*, which is a supernatural sensation of being touched by God deep in the center of the soul. The second is *flights of the spirit*, which refers to overpowering impulses of love that fill the soul with a consuming thirst for God. These flights can even send the body into an ecstatic trance. The third is *fiery darts of love*, which is a feeling of being pierced by divine charity. This ignites within us such a burning desire for God that we begin to hate whatever obstacles keep us from him. The fourth is called *wounds of love*. John of the Cross describes this as an "immense

...nt and yearning to see God." In a sense, these wounds afflict us more ...satisfy us because they greatly increase our appetite to gaze upon the Lord ...out bringing us to the full vision we yearn for.

Lesson Introduction

While in the Prayer of Union God takes over the internal senses, in the Prayer of Conforming Union, he takes over completely. He brings both internal and external faculties and senses under control.

Called Spiritual Betrothal by St. Teresa of Avila, this is the stage at which we are in final preparation for complete union with Our Lord. In fact, Fr. Jordan Aumann says that in this stage, the soul is already divinized.

Notes

What the Saints Say

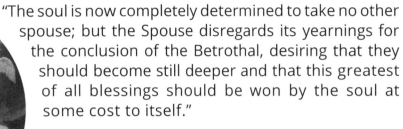

"The soul is now completely determined to take no other spouse; but the Spouse disregards its yearnings for the conclusion of the Betrothal, desiring that they should become still deeper and that this greatest of all blessings should be won by the soul at some cost to itself."

ST. TERESA OF AVILA — *16th century Spanish Mystic and Doctor of the Church*

Lectio Divina

"All night long on my bed
  I looked for the one my heart loves;
  I looked for him but did not find him.
I will get up now and go about the city,
  through its streets and squares;
I will search for the one my heart loves.
  So I looked for him but did not find him.
The watchmen found me
  as they made their rounds in the city.
  "Have you seen the one my heart loves?"

SONG OF SOLOMON 3:1-3

Meditation

It is perhaps a bit disconcerting that even at this level of prayer, Conforming Union (i.e., Spiritual Betrothal), suffering remains. And yet we all know that as long as we are on earth, suffering is a part of our lived experience. We can't escape it.

What we have to realize is that in the higher grades of prayer, our suffering is transformed. It is more closely united to the sufferings of Christ for the simple reason that *we* are more united to Christ.

So, there's a sense in which our suffering has achieved a redemptive value and power that it didn't have previously. Why? Because our acts of the will, "Here, Lord, I give this suffering to you", are now more under his control. We have almost given ourselves totally over to him. We have been, says Fr. Aumann, "fully divinized" (though not to the same degree that can happen only in heaven).

As such, the suffering we endure, we endure more willingly...just like Jesus Christ.

And though it's perhaps difficult to fully wrap our minds around, it's an interior and exterior suffering of *desire*. As Teresa says in the Sixth Mansion of the Interior Castle, "this is a great grief, though a sweet and delectable one; even if it should desire not to suffer it, it would have no choice – but, in any case, it never would so desire. It is much more satisfying to a soul than is the delectable absorption, devoid of distress, which occurs in the Prayer of Quiet" (chap. 2).

In other words, along with St. Paul, we can truly exclaim, "Now I rejoice in my sufferings for your sake, and in my flesh I complete what is lacking in Christ's afflictions for the sake of his body, that is, the church" (Col 1:24). And yet, as we're going to see, we still have yet to *fully* give ourselves over to the Lord.

Review Questions

1. Why does suffering continue to play a role in our spiritual development, even in the Prayer of Conforming Union? What kind of suffering is it?

2. What distinguishes the Prayer of Conforming Union from the Prayer of Union? Over what faculties does God now begin to exercise control?

3. How does Mary's betrothal to Joseph help us to understand what's going on?

4. What are the two basic forms of ecstasies, according to the video? How do the Saints and mystics describe them?

5. Why does God take over our external senses and "shut us down", so to speak, in this level of conforming union?

Discussion Questions

1. In this study, the Eighth Grade of prayer is called the Prayer of Conforming Union. St. Teresa, however, describes it as our "Spiritual Betrothal" with the Lord. Does her marital language help or hinder your understanding of our movement toward union with God?

2. Catholic teaching is clear that our souls have greater value and dignity than our bodies. Yet at the same time, the human person is a union of the two. The body is not simply a shell that contains the soul and that God plans to discard at the end of our lives. On the contrary, at the end of time our bodies are to be raised in glory and transformed. We will have both body and soul in eternity.

How does God's captivation of the bodily senses affirm the dignity and importance of the body? How much of us does he want for himself?

Prayer Journal

LESSON THIRTEEN

Prayer of Conforming Union, Part II – Betrothed to the Cross

What We Covered in Our Last Lesson

Last time we began our study of the Prayer of Conforming Union, the eighth of the Nine Grades of Prayer. This is the next-to-last stage that St. Teresa describes as our "Spiritual Betrothal" with the Lord. And as we discovered, the Prayer of Conforming Union is very closely related to the Prayer of Union. The two are part of the same level of prayer. They differ not in kind but in degree of intensity. Still, even at this advanced stage of communion with God, suffering continues to play a role. Despite the ecstasies now enjoyed, one is not yet in complete and permanent union with the Lord in heaven.

We also learned that, in the Prayer of Conforming Union, the Lord extends his reach over us even more. In the Prayer of Union, he captivated all of our interior faculties—our intellect, will, memory, imagination, etc. Only the bodily senses were free and untouched. In the Prayer of Conforming Union, however, God takes over completely. Even our exterior, bodily senses are brought under his loving control. The Lord is in the driver's seat, so to speak, and we are like putty in his hands.

Furthermore, we discovered there are two basic kinds of ecstasy at this level of prayer. Some are delightful and some are painful, yet both are directly connected with the Lord's intense love for us, and ours for him.

Delightful ecstasies tend to come on gradually. These are times of union with God that bring wonderful sensations of sweetness and make the soul realize how miserable the things of this world are in comparison with him. *Painful* ecstasies, by contrast, brings experiences of acute bodily suffering. Strange as it seems, the body can even become cold and appear as if dead. Of course, we always have to remember that the suffering we endure is driven by intense love. It is not something to fear. It's the result of living at a whole new level of relationship with God.

You'll also recall that St. Teresa of Avila breaks this down further and speaks of five different types of ecstasy. The first type, called *Ecstasy*, is when the soul seems to lose contact with its surroundings and is drawn to God alone.

The second, called *Rapture*, is when a sudden light shines from the Lord in the very depth of the soul that seems to separate the soul from the body. The third, called *Flights of the Spirit*, is nearly impossible to explain beyond the fact that something swift and subtle rises to the higher part of the soul and goes wherever the Lord wills. Extraordinary things such as bodily levitation can occur in these moments as well. The fourth type, called *Ecstatic Impulse*, is when one suddenly remembers that the soul is absent from God. And the fifth type, called *The Wound of Love*, is when the soul is consumed with desire and feels itself pierced by a fiery arrow of Divine Love.

All of these are amazing and beautiful gifts that unite us with God. They're the final preparations of "Spiritual Betrothal" that the Lord brings about in us before leading us to the "Spiritual Marriage."

Lesson Introduction

It's hard to ignore that even at this level of ecstatic prayer, there remains an element of suffering. That's because we're being wedded to the Cross of Christ, betrothed in the wedding supper of the Lamb that was slain.

And yet, more than ever, what we understand and experience is that the Cross is not something to be avoided. Our life has been radically transformed. It has been incredibly elevated. Christ is beginning to truly reveal that complete gift of self in union with him is the purest path to fulfillment and joy.

Notes

What the Saints Say

"I desire to suffer, Lord, because Thou didst suffer."

ST. TERESA OF AVILA — *16th century Spanish Mystic and Doctor of the Church*

Lectio Divina

"My beloved put his hand to the latch,
    and my heart was thrilled within me.
I arose to open to my beloved,
    and my hands dripped with myrrh,
my fingers with liquid myrrh,
    upon the handles of the bolt.
I opened for my beloved,
    but my beloved had left; he was gone.
    My heart sank at his departure.
I looked for him but did not find him.
    I called him but he did not answer.
The watchmen found me
    as they made their rounds in the city.
They beat me, they bruised me;
    they took away my cloak,
    those watchmen of the walls!
Daughters of Jerusalem, I charge you—
    if you find my beloved,
what will you tell him?
    Tell him I am faint with love."

SONG OF SONGS 5:6–8

Meditation

While many read the Song of Songs as nothing more than love poetry or literary drama, Teresa of Avila and John of the Cross see it as so much more. For them, as we've seen, the Bride and Bridegroom are analogous to the soul's relationship with our Bridegroom, Jesus Christ.

In other words, the Song of Songs is a poetic description of our desperate search for union with God.

And what's interesting is that as you read through chapter 5, it seems almost as if the Bridegroom is toying with the bride. He puts his hand to the door and causes her heart to race. "Hark! my beloved is knocking. 'Open to me, my sister, my love, my dove, my perfect one; for my head is wet with dew, my locks with the drops of the night'" (v. 2).

(An interesting aside is that the famous line in Revelation 3:20 where the Lord says, "Behold, I stand at the door and knock…" is an allusion back to this passage in Song of Songs.)

And yet, even though he comes to the door, he suddenly disappears into the night and the Bride has to go looking for him. Thinking they are on the cusp of consummating their love, she is in anguish at his departure. And as we've pointed out in another course in the Science of Sainthood about the Dark Night of the Soul, the Bride goes off into the night in search, even suffering at the hands of the watchmen. "They beat me, they wounded me…" (v. 7). Even so, she tells her friends that if they find her beloved, "tell him I am sick with love" (v. 8).

All of this is akin to our experience in Spiritual Betrothal, or the Prayer of Conforming Union. We think we're absolutely ready for spiritual marriage, but Christ holds off. He makes us wait a little longer, increasing our desire for him to the point that we're ready and willing to embrace the nighttime of suffering love like our Lord in his tragically beautiful Passion.

Review Questions

1. Why does the Lord "disregard the yearnings" of one who has reached the Prayer of Conforming Union? In other words, why does he hold us off when we so desperately desire union with him?

2. Why do we say that "union with the Cross fully happens" in the Prayer of Conforming Union?

3. What incredible mystical experience did both St. Teresa and St. Catherine of Siena experience at this stage of prayer?

4. What are the two passages of Scripture mentioned in the video that describe our relationship with Christ in terms of Betrothal and Marriage? How do both passages underscore the importance of suffering love?

Discussion Questions

1. While it's completely natural to experience some fear at the notion of suffering at this stage of prayer, don't forget that not only are we talking about suffering love, but also that God never asks us to do something without giving us the strength to do it. Can you think of other situations in life in which you knew suffering might occur, but persevered anyway?

2. The Church teaches that the Holy Spirit is the love that proceeds between the Father and the Son. It's his identity, so to speak. And in the Prayer of Conforming Union, Matthew says: "We're wading into the stream of that same, divinizing flow of love...that offers itself up completely for the other members of the Divine Family."

Does this understanding of the Holy Spirit and the fact that you are destined to become a member of this Divine Family help you understand what is happening at this point in the spiritual life?

3. During the Last Supper, Jesus gave us a golden key for unlocking the mystery of the Cross. He said: "Greater love has no man than this, that a man lay down his life for his friends" (John 15:13). He wants his disciples to see that the Cross is first and foremost an act of heroic love. In fact, he's telling us that the sacrifice of one's life is the most intense and most complete expression of love that is possible in a human nature. It's when *everything* is given for another and *nothing* is held back for oneself.

How would you describe the difference between sentimental love as idolized by the world and sacrificial love as advocated by Jesus? What does this tell us about the highest levels of prayer?

Prayer Journal

LESSON FOURTEEN

Prayer of Transforming Union – Entering Second Heaven

What We Covered in Our Last Lesson

In the last lesson, we deepened our understanding of the Prayer of Conforming Union, the eighth of the Nine Grades of Prayer that St. Teresa of Avila calls Spiritual Betrothal. We learned that this level of communion with God is both exhilarating and excruciating. It's exhilarating due to the ecstatic experiences that God grants to the soul that is receiving this final preparation for Spiritual Marriage. But it's also excruciating because we are passing through the final stage of the Dark Night of the Soul. We are being joined to the Cross of Christ and being submerged in the mystery of sacrificial love like never before.

In other words, we discovered that the ecstasies of Conforming Union are also painful on a deep level. The soul is yearning for union with the Divine Spouse, and yet God holds off. He disregards these yearnings in order to deepen them still more. His desire is to teach the soul that his greatest blessings cannot be won without cost. And what is that cost? Union with the Cross. Conformity to the sacrificial love of the crucified Christ.

In a sense, the soul enters the mystery of Jesus's cry of dereliction from the Cross: "My God, my God, why hast Thou forsaken me?" As St. Teresa describes this state, one is overcome by a deep sense of loneliness and total abandonment. So even though we are closer to God than ever, our experience is distinctly bittersweet.

So on one hand, the soul realizes that nothing in creation can provide the companionship it desperately desires. On the other, it senses that spousal union with the Lord is not possible without dying. Being suspended between heaven and earth, it has no idea what to do. The experience is reminiscent of St. Paul's declaration in Philippians 1:21, "For to me to live is Christ, and to die is gain...I am hard pressed between the two."

We were also reminded that espousal to Christ is revealed in Scripture. When the Saints speak of spiritual betrothal and marriage, they are neither clever innovators nor poets with overactive imaginations. They are speaking the language of biblical revelation. Saint Paul in Ephesians 5:22–27, for example, describes the relationship between Christ and the Church as that of a husband and wife, a bridegroom and bride. Likewise, the climax of the Book of Revelation announces the wedding supper of the Lamb (Rev 19:6–9). This is what is waiting for the people of God at the end. This is the blessing won by the Lamb who sacrificed himself in love because he desires nothing less than an indissoluble bond of union with us.

The highpoint of the Prayer of Conforming Union, then, is our betrothal to Christ. It's the final step in prayer as we begin to transition to mystical marriage. That's why the feeling of abandonment, combined with our yearning for his Presence, pains us more than anything we can imagine. We desire God more than anything else and have yet to be satisfied.

Lesson Introduction

The final grade of St. Teresa's Nine Grades of Prayer is the Prayer of Transforming Union, which she calls Spiritual Marriage. And while the lines between these highest grades of prayer may often seem a little blurry, she explains that this level is far beyond all previous ones. It is truly a foretaste of heaven and a prelude to the Beatific Vision itself.

Notes

_____

_____

_____

_____

_____

_____

_____

What the Saints Say

"Arise, make haste my love… The bride feels that this voice of the Bridegroom speaking within her is the end of evil and the beginning of good. In the refreshment, protection, and delightful sentiment afforded by this voice, she too, like the sweet nightingale, sings a new and jubilant song together with God, who moves her to do this. He gives his voice to her that so united with him she may give it together with him to God."

ST. JOHN OF THE CROSS — *16th century Spanish Mystic and Doctor of the Church*

Lectio Divina

"My beloved spoke and said to me,
  'Arise, my darling,
  my beautiful one, come with me.
See! The winter is past;
  the rains are over and gone.
Flowers appear on the earth;
  the season of singing has come,
the cooing of doves
  is heard in our land.
The fig tree forms its early fruit;
  the blossoming vines spread their fragrance.
Arise, come, my darling;
  my beautiful one, come with me.'"

SONG OF SONGS 2:10–13

Meditation

Practically speaking, what does transformation in Christ consist of on this side of heaven? It's an important question because it's easy to get caught up into lofty discussions of divinization and participation in the divine nature of God, and so lose the forest for the trees.

Of course, this is totally understandable. After all, who wouldn't want to focus on what John of the Cross describes as "so sublime, delicate, and deep a delight that a mortal tongue finds it indescribable" (*The Spiritual Canticle* Stanza 39)?

But as we've discussed in the last few lessons, once we attain the highest union with God possible while still on earth, supernatural ecstasies and raptures essentially cease. Yes, we're intimately participating in the divine nature, but we've become so much like God that his presence doesn't now cause the same kind of disruption in our body and soul, disruptions that tend to draw our attention.

So again, is there a different, more "practical" manner of speaking about all of this that helps to illuminate what is happening? Yes. And as usual, the answer, at least a good deal of it, comes from the pen of St. Teresa of Avila. Practical perfection, she says, essentially consists of being conformed to the will of God.

"The highest perfection consists not in interior favors or in great raptures or in visions or in the spirit of prophecy, but in the bringing of our wills so closely into conformity with the will of God that, as soon as we realize he wills anything, we desire it ourselves with all our might, and take the bitter with the sweet, knowing that to be His Majesty's will" (*Book of Foundations* Chapter 5).

Put simply, spiritual growth and becoming like God results in the union of *our* will with the perfect will of *God*. That's divine participation in a nutshell. The practical goal of the spiritual life is all about trustful surrender to Divine Providence on every single level and in every single aspect of this life...period.

As Christ himself prayed to the Father, "Not as I will, but as thou wilt" (Matthew 26:39).

Review Questions

1. What is unique about the Ninth Grade of prayer, the Prayer of Transforming Union? How does it differ from the Eighth Grade of prayer, the Prayer of Conforming Union?

2. St. Teresa of Avila describes the Transforming Union as an "intellectual vision" of the Trinity that does not involve either the senses or the imagination. What does she mean by this?

3. While the experience of Transforming Union is essentially beyond words, spiritual writers indicate this is also when ecstasies basically cease. We don't experience the same kind of supernatural phenomena that we did earlier. Why is this the case?

4. Can you name the three common elements that accompany the Transforming Union, according to St. John of the Cross?

Discussion Questions

1. From earliest times Christians have believed that grace makes us "partakers of the divine nature" (2 Peter 1:4). This summarizes a long process of transformation that begins in Baptism and reaches its highest degree (this side of heaven) in the Prayer of Transforming Union. It's the goal of the entire Christian life, yet shockingly few Catholics have ever heard of "divinization."

If someone had previously asked you what disciples of Christ should ultimately be striving for, what would you have said? What would you say now?

2. At first glance, it's astounding to think that every Christian without exception is invited into the incredible, unfathomable depths of the God through dedicated prayer. On further reflection, however, it makes complete sense since every Christian is ultimately called to enter and enjoy the Beatific Vision of God in heaven.

Were you fully aware of this incredible reality before working through the present study? How does this goal change the way you think about prayer, and more importantly, how you practice it?

3. Has what you've learned in this study changed your understanding of what it means to be part of God's family? Has it increased your desire to focus more upon your spiritual life and draw closer to God?

Prayer Journal

Summary of Lesson Fourteen

The Prayer of Transforming Union is the highest degree of perfection that a person can attain on this side of heaven. Fr. Jordan Aumann calls it a "prelude to the beatific life of glory." St. John of the Cross goes even further saying that we are "transformed into God by love," and we are "more divine than human" at this point.

In the language of St. Teresa of Avila, this level is called Spiritual Marriage, in which we are united to God to the highest degree possible on earth. And in this new level of union, we experience an intellectual vision of God through which he impresses himself upon us in a way that goes beyond all previous vision or spiritual consolation. It is a new, constant companionship with the Most Holy Trinity that almost defies description.

St. John of the Cross says there are three common elements that accompany the Prayer of Transforming Union: transformation in God, mutual surrender, and the permanent union of love.

Once a soul reaches this level, we are united to God in a bond that is virtually unbreakable. While we always retain our freewill, St. John of the Cross says that we are "confirmed in grace" and the odds of us forsaking the Lord are slim to none.

At this stage, the soul is fully abandoned to the will of God. No longer in fear of hardship or suffering of any kind, it is supremely confident in St. Paul's words in Romans 8:28 that "We know that in everything God works for good with those who love him."

And while what has been described in this study may seem out of reach, we can never forget that union with God is exactly what each one of us is created for. God has a plan for every single person and will give us the grace we need to progress in prayer as far he desires and experience him in the manner he deems most perfect for us as his child. Our job is to seek him with every ounce of strength we have and receive the incredible life he has prepared for us, both now and forever.

SCIENCE *of* SAINTHOOD

Ready to continue climbing the divine ladder toward God?

Join the Science of Sainthood today and experience a whole level of prayer and divine intimacy!

"Blown away"

"I can hardly believe how wonderful this is."

Head over to **ScienceofSainthood.com**, scroll to the bottom, and choose your plan!

Courses in the Science of Sainthood include:

- ◆ Introduction to Real Prayer
- ◆ The 7 Deadly Sins
- ◆ The Moral Virtues
- ◆ The Theological Virtues
- ◆ The Dark Night of the Soul
- ◆ The Unitive Way & Deeper Prayer
- ◆ St. Teresa of Avila's 9 Grades of Prayer
- ◆ The Gifts of the Spirt ...*and more!*

Join Catholics from all over the globe in one of the world's premiere online schools of authentic Catholic spiritual formation! More than education, it's transformation!

"If you've ever wanted to deepen your life of prayer and actually make some progress in avoiding vice and growing in virtue, then look no further. The Science of Sainthood is for you."

Dr. Brant Pitre – Renowned theologian & author of *Jesus and the Jewish Roots of the Eucharist*

ScienceofSainthood.com

Want more spiritual nourishment?

Check out **The Art of Catholic podcast**. Available on Youtube, iTunes, Spotify, Amazon, and more!

"A theological thrill ride!"

–*Mark Hart*, *Executive Vice-President of LifeTeen International*

"I invite you to sit down and begin reading a book that will not only inform you but transform you, your prayer, and your spiritual life in Christ."

–*Dr. Brant Pitre*, *Renowned Author of* Jesus & the Jewish Roots of the Eucharist

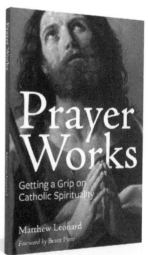

Made in the USA
Columbia, SC
02 February 2022

55303127R00054